A LANGUAGE LEARNING ADVENTURE

GOODBYE USA
Bonjour la France

Anne Elizabeth Bovaird
Illustrated by Pierre Ballouhey

BARRON'S

"Scat cat, I'm trying to read!" said Tom looking at a picture book of Paris.

"Listen to this, Mom. The book says that Paris is very old and there are lots of interesting things to see. For instance, the Eiffel Tower is the tallest building in Paris. There are 1,652 steps up to the top. And Notre Dame is a cathedral built on an island in the middle of the city!"

Next week Tom is going to France to visit his cousin Pierre, Aunt Nicole, and Uncle Jacques in Paris for the first time.

Tom's dad is taking the plane with him as far as Paris. Then he is leaving Tom to go to an important business meeting.

"Does cousin Pierre speak English?" Tom asked. He picked up a picture of Pierre and his family and was trying to figure out if his cousin looked nice or not.

"Why no, Tom. Pierre's French and he speaks French."

"You mean he doesn't know any English! How can we be friends if I don't understand what he says!" Tom hadn't thought of this before now, and he was nervous about meeting someone he couldn't talk to.

"Not everyone in the world speaks English," Tom's mom replied.

Tom of course knew that. He knew kids at school who spoke Spanish. But he wasn't sure about making friends with someone from another country.

"Tell you what—I'll teach you some words in French. After all, Pierre's the same age as you. You have lots of things in common."

Tom's mom wrote down some expressions in English. Next to them, she wrote the same expressions in French.

"First of all, what do you notice about the English words and the French words?"

Tom looked at the list very carefully. A lot of words looked different, but some looked familiar. "Well, the words 'no,' 'table,' 'uncle,' and 'cousin' look the same or almost the same in French."

"That's right," Tom's mother agreed. "Some words do look the same, but they're pronounced differently. Let's draw a third column. When I say the word in French, you tell me what it sounds like in English."

"The first word is *Salut*. It means 'hello' or 'hi.'"

"Sa-lew," repeated Tom. "Well, the first part sounds like the word 'sat' without the T and the second part like the word 'few' but with an L instead of an F."

"Very good! So let's write sa(t) and lew and put parentheses around the letters we don't want to pronounce."

"I get it! Just pretend the T doesn't exist!"

"Now the second expression is *Ça va*. It means two things. It's a question, 'How's it going?' and an answer, 'Fine! Things are great!' *Ça va* is a kind of greeting used between two friends. What does it sound like in English?"

"The first part sounds like sa(t) and the second like va(t). Say them together fast and they mean 'How are things?' in French! And I answer back *Ça va!* 'Things are great!' "

Tom was quite happy with himself. French isn't half as complicated to learn as math!—And if you practice along with Tom, you can learn some French too!

"Okay. So now I know 13 expressions in French," explained Tom. "But what about all the other words I don't know? What do I say when I want to know what something is in French? Pierre's going to think I'm stupid!"

"No he won't," laughed his mother. "When you want to know what a word is in French, just ask him. 'What is it?' in French is *Qu'est-ce que c'est?*."

"Kess ca(t) say," repeated Tom. "It sounds like kess, cat, say, except without the T!"

"Now it's my turn. Let me try to speak French," said Tom excitedly. "*Qu'est-ce c'est*, Mom? See this model airplane Dad gave me? It's a big 747 jet, like the one I'm going to take to France."

"The word 'plane' is *avion* in French. *C'est un avion* means 'it's a plane.'"

"Say tuh a(t)-V-on. Hey, I'm speaking French!"

"And this is a present for your *Tante Nicole* and *Oncle Jacques*. In French, a present is *cadeau*."

"Ca(t)-doe. *C'est un cadeau*," sang Tom. "It's a present!"

The night before his trip, Tom went to bed dreaming about France. He wondered what French kids do for fun. Do they have toy trains and racing cars? Do they ride bikes and roller skate? Do they play baseball?

The new French words he had learned ran round and round in his head. See if you can match the French words with the English.

The next day Tom woke up and went down for breakfast.

"*Bonjour*, Mom," he shouted. "*Ça va?*"

"*Bonjour*, Tom. *Ça va!*" answered his mom. She was making a special meal before his trip.

"After breakfast we'll finish packing, and I'm going to take an *avion* today, and see the Eiffel Tower, and give *Tante Nicole* a *cadeau,* and say *salut* to Pierre and . . ."

"Not so fast! Finish your breakfast first," said Tom's dad.

At the airport, Tom had to show his passport at the ticket counter. The passport says that he is American and was born in Chicago.

The woman who took his ticket explained that the plane ride took eight hours and that Paris was 4,500 miles (or 7,240 kilometers) away. The plane had to fly over New York, cross the Atlantic Ocean, and pass over England before arriving at Charles de Gaulle Airport in Paris.

When it was time to get on the plane, Tom suddenly felt sad. He put his arms around his mother and gave her a big hug.

"Be good, Tom," said his mom. "And remember, Pierre is just like your friends back here in Chicago. Call me tomorrow night when you arrive."

"*Oui*, Mom. I will. *Au revoir!*"

"*Au revoir Tom!*"

Tom and his dad placed their bags on a conveyor belt to be X-rayed.

"Security checks are very important," Tom's dad explained.

On the plane, the stewardess gave Tom a landing card to fill out. She explained that he would have to give it to the immigration officer in Paris. All foreigners traveling to France are required to do this. Tom had never thought of himself as a foreigner before.

The card was written in both French and English, and some of the French words looked familiar—for example, 'name' and *nom*, 'date' and *date*, 'nationality' and *nationalité*.

Tom remembered what his mom said about some French words looking like English words. Boy, she sure knows a lot!

At Charles de Gaulle Airport, Tom said goodbye to his dad. He was so excited to be in Paris that he forgot to feel sad!

Tom followed the other passengers to the immigration counter and waited his turn.

"*Bonjour*," said Tom to the officer behind the counter.

"*Bonjour*," answered the man without looking up. He took Tom's landing card and stamped his passport.

"*Au revoir*," said Tom.

"*Au revoir*," said the man.

"I did it," thought Tom. "I spoke French and he understood me!"

Tom walked out into the arrival lounge and looked around. All around him people were speaking French. They talked so quickly that Tom only recognized a few words.

"I'm not afraid of all these people," thought Tom. But he was, just a little.

"Hey wait a minute! There's someone holding up a sign with my name on it!"

"*Bienvenue Tom!* I'm your *Tante Nicole.*"

"Bee-N-ve-new?" repeated Tom.

"That means 'Welcome. We're so glad you could come!' "

"*Tante Nicole, c'est un cadeau,*" said Tom, holding out the present.

"Oh Tom, *merci.*"

"And this is your *cousin, Pierre*."

Tom looked at Pierre.
Pierre looked at Tom.

He seems like an ordinary kid, Tom thought. He's got the same kind of hair as me and is the same size as me. Only difference is he's wearing glasses and is dressed up.

"*Salut, Tom. Ça va?*" asked Pierre politely.

"*Salut, Pierre. Ça va!*" answered Tom.

Tom held out his hand to Pierre.

All of a sudden, Pierre reached over and kissed Tom on both cheeks.

"Hey, cut that out!" said Tom. "I'm not a girl!"

Pierre looked hurt. "*Désolé, Tom*," he said.

"Day-so-lay?" repeated Tom.

"*Désolé* means sorry, Tom. In France we often kiss each other on the cheek when we meet," explained *Tante Nicole*. "Pierre just wanted you to feel welcome."

"I . . . I'm sorry. . .I mean *désolé,*" Tom said. "You see, we don't do that in Chicago. We usually just shake hands."

Tom held his hand out again to Pierre. He felt terrible. He hoped Pierre didn't think he was mean or unfriendly.

But Pierre didn't seem to mind. He took Tom's hand and smiled.

On the way home from the airport they drove past a huge white church on top of a hill. The roof was round instead of pointed like the ones back home. Tom thought he recognized it from somewhere. Well, the only way he was going to find out was by asking.

"*Qu'est ce que c'est, Pierre?*" said Tom, hoping his cousin would understand.

"*Ah Tom, c'est Sacré Coeur!*" answered Pierre.

"*C'est* sack-ray ker. I get it! Now I remember. It's *Sacré Coeur*. I saw it in the picture book I have about Paris!"

Pierre laughed and nodded his head.

Pierre lived in an apartment in the city—not in a house in the suburbs like Tom.

When they arrived, Pierre took Tom to see his room and unpack. It really wasn't much different from Tom's room back home. There were two beds, a table, and some toys. Tom sat down on one of the beds and started bouncing.

"*Qu'est-ce que c'est?*" asked Tom between bounces.

"*C'est un lit*," answered Pierre, watching him curiously.

"*C'est* uh lee," repeated Tom. "It's a bed."

Tom looked around the room pointing to things and asking Pierre what they were in French.

Do you understand what Pierre is saying? Look at the French words and pictures and help Tom figure out what the words mean in English.

Tom started to unpack his suitcase. He took out his baseball, and bat, and he handed them to Pierre.

"*Qu'est-ce que c'est, Tom?*"

"*C'est un* baseball," answered Tom proudly. "You mean to tell me you've never played baseball? Why, baseball is the greatest game in the whole wide world! See my cap, the Chicago Cubs, that's my team!"

Pierre looked a little confused.

Pierre reached under his bed and pulled out a soccer ball.

Showing it to Tom, he said, "*C'est un ballon de football*."

"*Non!* That's not a football, *c'est un* soccer ball!" groaned Tom. He was really mixed up. His cousin didn't even know the difference between a soccer ball and a football.

"In France, our national sport is football. I think you call it soccer in America," said a man leaning against the bedroom door.

"*Papa*," cried Pierre. "*C'est Tom!*"

"You must be my Uncle Jacques," said Tom excitedly. "*Bonjour Oncle Jacques. Ça va?*"

"*Bonjour Tom. Ça va!* I see you two are getting acquainted. Why don't you take your ball and bat and go play in the park until dinner. Pierre will show you around the neighborhood."

Pierre led Tom outside the apartment. Tom was curious to see what a French neighborhood looked like. As they started to walk down the street, he saw a woman pushing a baby stroller.

"*Qu'est-ce c'est, Pierre?*"

"*C'est un bébé.*" Pierre held up one finger and pointed to the baby.

"Uh bay-bay," repeated Tom. "One baby."

Further down the street, Pierre pointed to two policemen dressed in blue uniforms standing on a corner. They looked very important.

"*Qu'est-ce que c'est, Pierre?*"

"*Deux agents de police.*"

"Duh a(t)-jan duh po-lease," repeated Tom. "Two policemen. Hey Pierre, how do you count to ten in French? You know, one, two, three . . ."

Tom held up ten fingers to help Pierre understand what he wanted.

And he did understand!

Pierre pointed to three cats sitting on a window ledge and said "*trois chats*."

"Trwa sha(t)" repeated Tom. "Three cats. *Un, deux, trois*."

"*Quatre arbres*," continued Pierre.

"Catra arbra, four trees," sang Tom. He liked this game.

On their way to the park, Pierre taught Tom how to count to ten.

Can you help Tom learn to count?

un bébé
[uh bay-bay]   one baby

deux agents de police   two policeman
[duh a (t)-jan duh po-lease]

trois chats   three cats
[trwa sha(t)]

quatre arbres   four trees
[catra arbra]

cinq voitures   five cars
[sank vwa-tewr]

six chiens   six dogs
[cease she-N]

sept filles   seven girls
[set fee]

huit garçons   eight boys
[wheat gar-son]

neuf oiseaux   nine birds
[nuhf wa-zoe]

dix francs   ten Francs
[dees fran(k)]

When they arrived at the park, Tom recognized some of the things he had seen with Pierre.

He saw some: *bébés*, *chiens*, *filles*, *garçons*, *chats*, *arbres*, and *oiseaux*.

Can you find them too?
How many of each do you see?

The two boys found an open spot on the grass. Tom took out his
baseball bat and gave it to Pierre.

"Now, I'm going to throw the ball. You watch it carefully and try to hit it,"
explained Tom.

Pierre didn't look too sure of himself, but nodded just the same.
He bravely lifted the bat.

Tom threw the ball and . . .

. . . Pierre missed.

"*Désolé Tom*," said Pierre turning red. He was really discouraged.

"Don't be sorry, we'll try again. You can do it! You're my cousin, aren't you!" said Tom.

Tom threw another ball, and another, and another.

Finally, Pierre hit one . . .

. . . smack into a flower bed!

"Good hit!" yelled Tom, jumping up and down. "Your aim is a little off, but it was a great first try."

"*Merci, Tom!*" replied Pierre.

Both boys walked to the flower bed.

"I see it! It's over here, next to the red flowers," indicated Tom.

"*Non Tom, les fleurs jaunes,*" insisted Pierre, standing near some yellow flowers.

"*Qu'est-ce que c'est* lay fluhr joan?" asked Tom.

Pierre picked some yellow flowers and handed them to Tom.

"Ah, I get it, *fleur* means 'flower' and *jaune* means 'yellow,' " said Tom excitedly.

"And these?" asked Tom, bending down to pick some red flowers.

"*Les fleurs rouges*," answered Pierre.

"Rooj, red, *rouge*," repeated Tom. "And these other colors—white, green, orange, blue, and violet? How do you say them in French?" Tom's bunch of flowers was growing bigger and bigger.

"*Blanc, vert, orange, bleu, et violet*," explained Pierre.

"Blan(k), ver, O-ranj, bluh, V-O-lay, why some of these colors are almost the same in English!"

"I found it!" cried Tom, holding up the lost baseball.

But Pierre wasn't listening. He was looking over Tom's shoulder at something and seemed pretty worried about what he saw.

"*Qu'est-ce que vous faites ici!*" a voice boomed out.

Tom turned around and found himself standing face to face with *un agent de police.*

"*Désolé, Monsieur*," said Pierre nervously.

"*Désolé* me(t)-sewer," repeated Tom, trying to hide the flowers behind his back. "But you see we were playing baseball, and my cousin hit the ball too hard, and . . ."

The *agent de police* did not seem impressed.

Suddenly, Tom had an idea.

"*C'est un cadeau*," he said, holding out the bunch of flowers to the policeman.
Then Tom put on his best smile, the one that always worked when he got in
trouble at home.

The *agent de police* took the flowers and scratched his head. Just as he opened his mouth to speak, Tom grabbed Pierre by the sleeve and started to back away.

"*Au revoir, Monsieur,*" yelled Tom.

And with that, the two boys ran out of the park.

On their way home, they stopped to catch their breath. Luckily, the policeman wasn't following them.

"Did you see the look on his face when I gave him the flowers?" Tom imitated The *agent de police* for Pierre.

Pierre took one look at Tom and burst out laughing. Soon both boys were in hysterics.

Inside the apartment, Aunt Nicole sent Tom and Pierre to their room to get ready for dinner.

Tom felt happy. He was having a great time in Paris and Pierre really wasn't that different from his friends back home after all. It didn't matter that Tom couldn't speak French very well, and that Pierre couldn't speak English. He was still his friend.

Tom took off his baseball cap and handed it to Pierre.

"*C'est un cadeau.*"

"*Pour moi? Oh Tom, merci!*" exclaimed Pierre.

The two boys stood side by side in front of a mirror while Pierre took off his glasses and tried on his new cap.

But wait a minute! Who is who? That's not Pierre anymore. The baseball cap had transformed Pierre into Tom!

Tom had another great idea. "Pierre, let's play a joke on your mom and dad!"

He took off his shirt and handed it to Pierre. "Now give me your shirt."

Pierre slowly began to smile. He understood what Tom wanted him to do.

"*À table!* Dinner's ready!" called *Tante Nicole* from the dining room.

Five minutes later both boys walked into the dining room.

"Tom, you sit here next to me," offered *Tante Nicole*.

She turned to Pierre and explained something to him quickly in French.

Pierre didn't move. He just stood there smiling.

"Pierre, please do what your mother asked," said *Oncle Jacques*. He was getting rather annoyed.

Both boys suddenly started to laugh.

"*Maman, Papa, c'est Tom*," explained the fake Tom pointing to the real Tom.

"I'm not Pierre, *Tante Nicole* and *Oncle Jacques*. I'm Tom! That's Pierre, he's just wearing my clothes!" shouted the fake Pierre pointing to the real Pierre. "We really fooled you, didn't we!"

Tante Nicole and *Oncle Jacques* started to laugh too. "Well, Tom, it looks like you're practically French now."

"No, I'm not. I'm American!" said Tom, "but I'm learning French fast!"

After dinner, Tom phoned his mom.

"Paris is great, Mom. I saw *Sacré Coeur* today. And I learned how to count to ten, and the names of colors. And we played baseball in the park. And Mom, you were right about Pierre. He's not so different from me. I understand him, even if I don't know how to say lots of things in French. But he's teaching me. I gotta go now . . . I love you too, Mom.

Au revoir!

Guide to French Pronunciation

Pronouncing French isn't always easy! That's why Tom must repeat every French word he hears. Whenever possible, he uses English words that sound the same as the French word to help him speak French like Pierre. Here is the "secret code" that Tom uses for representing the correct sound in French.

• When you see a capital letter, pronounce it as if you were reciting the alphabet.
> Example: *Violet*   V-O-lay

• When you see a letter in parentheses, pronounce the word as you would in English, but omit the letter that is enclosed by the parentheses.
> Example: *Une*   (j)une

• Nasals are special sounds pronounced in some French words. You can recognize a nasal when you see a vowel (a,e,i,o,u) followed by an N or an M in Tom's pronunciation code.
> Example: *Chien*   she-N

Tom has a lot of trouble saying nasals correctly. He usually stops just short of pronouncing the N or the M. (These sounds are called nasals because the sound comes through your nose when you say them.)

Glossary (French–English)

French	Pronunciation	English
A		
À table	a(t) ta(p)-bla	Come and get it!
Agent de police	a(t)-jan duh po-lease	Policeman
Arbres	arbra	Trees
Au revoir	or-vwar	Goodbye
Avion	a(t)-V-on	Plane
B		
Ballon de football	ba-lon duh foot-bal	Soccer ball
Bébé	bay-bay	Baby
Bienvenue	bee-N-ve-new	Welcome
Blanc	blan(k)	White
Bleu	bluh	Blue
Bonjour	bon-joor	Good day
Bureau	bew-row	Desk
C		
Ça va?	sa(t) va(t)	How's it going?
Ça va!	sa(t) va(t)	Things are fine!
Cadeau	ca(t)-doe	Present
C'est un/une…	say ton/say tune	It's a…
Chaise	shayz	Chair
Chats	sha(t)	Cats

Chiens	she-N	Dogs
Cinq	sank	Five
Cousin	coo-zan	Cousin

D

Date	da(d)-t	Date
Deux	duh	Two
Désolé	day-so-lay	Sorry
Dix	dees	Ten
Drapeau	dra-poe	Flag

F

Fenêtre	fe-netra	Window
Filles	fee	Girls
Fleurs	fluhr	Flowers
Francs	fran(k)	Francs

G

Garçons	gar-son	Boys

H

Huit	wheat	Eight

J

Jaune	joan	Yellow
Jouet	joo-ay	Toy

L

La	la	The (feminine)
Le	luh	The (masculine)
Lit	lee	Bed
Livre	leevra	Book

M

Maman	ma(t)-ma(t)	Mom
Merci	mer-see	Thank you
Moi	mwa	Me
Monsieur	me(t)-sewer	Sir

N

Nationalité	na-see-O-na-lee-tay	Nationality
Neuf	nuhf	Nine
Nom	nom	Name
Non	no	No
Notre Dame	no-tra dam	Notre Dame

O

Oiseaux	wa-zoe	Birds
Oncle	on-kla	Uncle
Orange	O-ranj	Orange
Oui	we	Yes

P

Papa	pa(t)-pa(t)	Dad
Pour	poor	For

Q

Quatre	catra	Four
Qu'est-ce que c'est?	kess ca(t) say	What is it?

R

Rouge	rooj	Red

S

Sacré Coeur	sack-ray ker	Sacred Heart
Salut	sa(t)-lew	Hi, Hello
Sept	set	Seven
S'il vous plaît	seal-voo-play	Please
Six	ceese	Six

T

Table	ta(p)-bla	Table
Tante	tant	Aunt
Tour Eiffél	tour F-L	Eiffel Tower
Trois	trwa	Three

U

Un	uh	One/A (masculine)
Une	(j)une	One/A (feminine)

V

Vert	ver	Green
Violet	V-O-lay	Violet
Voitures	vwa-tewr	Cars

This book is dedicated to Mom and Dad with love.
I had never thought about what it means to be
an American before living in France.

All inquiries should be addressed to:
Barron's Educational Series, Inc.
250 Wireless Boulevard
Hauppauge, NY 11788

International Standard Book No.   0-8120-6406-2 (hardcover)
                                   0-8120-4960-8 (paperback)

Library of Congress Catalog Card No. 93-13355

Library of Congress Cataloging-in-Publication Data

    (available upon request)

PRINTED IN HONG KONG
3456   9955   987654321